Dedications
—To Momtom, my mother. All that I am, I owe to you. Thank
you for everything, Helen.

—And to my mother Peg, with many thanks you's. Love from
Juliette.

Published in Great Britain in 1990 by Exley Publications Ltd.
Published simultaneously in 1992 by Exley Publications Ltd in
Great Britain, and Exley Giftbooks in the USA.
Second printing 1990
Third, fourth and fifth printings 1992
Illustrations © Exley Publications Ltd, 1990
Selection & Design © Helen Exley, 1990
ISBN 1-85015-214-4
Printed in Spain by Grafo S.A. – Bilbao.

Exley Publications Ltd, 16 Chalk Hill, Watford, Herts WD1 4BN,
United Kingdom.
Exley Giftbooks, 359 East Main Street, Suite 3D, Mount Kisco,
NY 10549, USA.

An illustrated

Mother's Notebook

illustrated by Juliette Clarke
and edited by Helen Exley

EXLEY

MT. KISCO, NEW YORK • WATFORD, UK

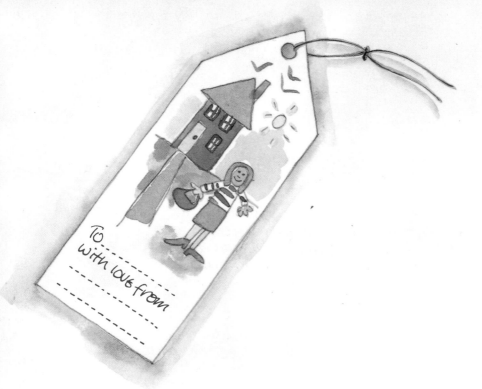

To - - - - - - - - -
with love from
- - - - - - - - - -
- - - - - - - - - -

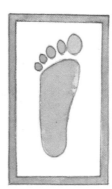

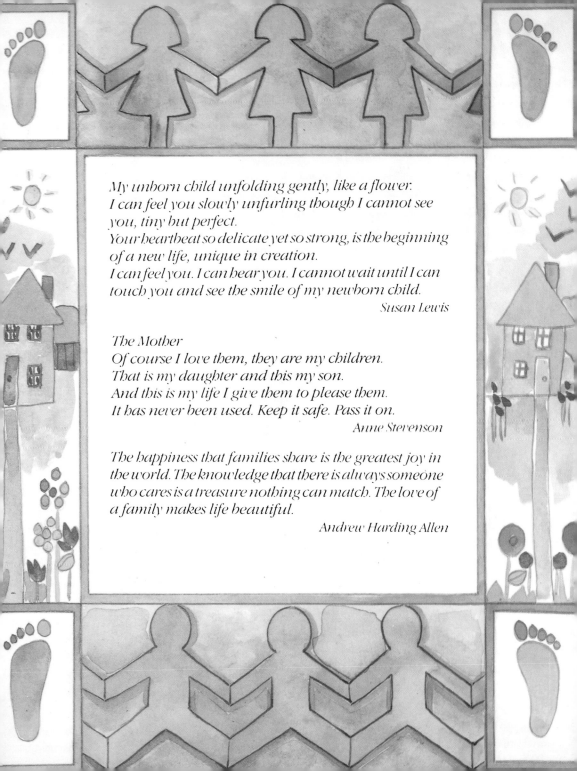

My unborn child unfolding gently, like a flower.
I can feel you slowly unfurling though I cannot see
you, tiny but perfect.
Your heartbeat so delicate yet so strong, is the beginning
of a new life, unique in creation.
I can feel you. I can hear you. I cannot wait until I can
touch you and see the smile of my newborn child.

Susan Lewis

The Mother
Of course I love them, they are my children.
That is my daughter and this my son.
And this is my life I give them to please them.
It has never been used. Keep it safe. Pass it on.

Anne Stevenson

The happiness that families share is the greatest joy in
the world. The knowledge that there is always someone
who cares is a treasure nothing can match. The love of
a family makes life beautiful.

Andrew Harding Allen

To Momtom
HAPPY
MOTHERS DAY
With all my
love Helen

With the approach of Mother's Day, the mob of
wild-eyed daughters progressing from shop to
shop are all looking for cards that just say
"Thanks, mom. I love you".

Peter Gray

My proudest pleasure is when my beautiful little three-year-old girl puts her arms around my neck, she squeezes me tight and says "I love you mummy, I really do."

A. Cooper

A mother understands what a child does not say.

Jewish proverb

There is nothing on earth like the moment of seeing one's first baby. Men scale other heights, but there is no height like this simple one, occurring continuously throughout all the ages in musty bedrooms, in palaces, in caves and desert places. I looked at this rolled-up bundle ... and knew again I had not created her. She was herself apart from me. She had her own life to lead, her own destiny to accomplish; she just came past me to this earth. My job was to get her to adulthood and then push her off.

Katherine Trevelyan

Mums are inclined to go out into the kitchen to make a pot of tea when the News repeats the story of the missing child, the famine, the earthquake. She is all those other mothers. And she is powerless.

Pam Brown

Every man, for the sake of the great blessed Mother in Heaven, and for the love of his own little mother on earth, should handle all womankind gently, and hold them in all honour.
Alfred Lord Tennyson

Lily of the ~Valley~

Flowers from April to may. Grows to 6-8 inches in height.

Forget-me-not.

Flowers from April-may. Grows to 6-12 inches in height.

I shall never forget my mother, for it was she who planted and nurtured the first seeds of Good within me. She opened my heart to the impressions of nature; she awakened my understanding and extended my horizon, and her precepts exerted an everlasting influence upon the course of my life.

Immanuel Kant

A mother's love! What can compare with it! Of all things on earth, it comes nearest to divine love in heaven.

A mother's love means a life's devotion – and sometimes a life's sacrifice – with but one thought, one hope and one feeling, that her children will grow up healthy and strong, free from evil habits and able to provide for themselves. Her sole wish is that they may do their part like men and women, avoid dangers and pitfalls, and when dark hours come, trust in Providence to give them strength, patience and courage to bear up bravely.

Happy is the mother when her heart's wish is answered, and happy are her sons and daughters when they can feel that they have contributed to her noble purpose and, in some measure, repaid her unceasing, unwavering love and devotion.

Anon

*Mothers are inclined to feel limp at fifty. This is because the
children have taken most of her stuffing to build their nests.*
Samantha Armstrong

Mums are not so much concerned about Education, Paediatrics, Child Poverty, Law and Order and the Arms Race as about Emily and Robert and Imram and Njoroge. Which is, after all, the same thing.

Clare D'Arcy

So Judith decided against ballet and became a clerk. And John, the teenage pacifist, joined the Navy. Patterns of childhood changed overnight as in a shaken kaleidoscope and you were left wondering if anything you ever said or did or tried for had any part in their making. But sometimes, unexpectedly, you'll hear them say something with firm conviction – and they are your words and it is your voice. Echoing down the years from a day half forgotten – a day of non-event, a day lost among other days. Children take what they need from us – not what we offer.

Pam Brown

*She is my first, great love. She was a wonderful, rare woman
—you do not know; as strong, and steadfast, and generous as
the sun. She could be as swift as a white whiplash, and as kind
and gentle as warm rain, and as steadfast as the irreducible
earth beneath us.*

D. H. Lawrence

A wife knows her husband only from the moment that their lives converged. Two strangers brought together by the chance of love, they will in part remain so until death or disillusion separate them once again: but in motherhood the woman discovers another kind of loving, for however time or circumstance may come between her and her child, their lives are interwoven forever. Willingly or unwillingly she has projected herself forward into Time, and will from now on, see the world through other eyes than her own.

Pam Brown

Some are kissing mothers and some are scolding mothers, but it is love just the same, and most mothers kiss and scold together.

Pearl Buck

*A mother is a woman
with a twenty-five hour day who can
still find an hour to play with her family.*
                                        Iris Peck

Giving advice comes naturally to mothers. Advice is in the
genes along with blue eyes and red hair.

Lois Wyse

Inside every elderly human being is a small child missing its mom.

Helen Thomson

As a mother bottles jam, ices a birthday cake, mends the toilet, splits the iris corms, diagnoses German measles, cuts the dog's claws, irons the dress shirt, cleans the carpet, replaces the guttering, disembowels the rabbit, knocks up a pirate costume at four hour's notice, corrects her child's French accent, placates the Insurance man, analyzes the character of Prospero and de-fleas the cat, she realizes sadly that she is totally without qualifications and will have the option of shop work or house cleaning once the kids leave home. She could, of course, take an extra mural degree. In between.

Pam Brown

Kindness is contagious. The spirit of harmony trickles down by a thousand secret channels into the inmost recesses of the household life. One truly affectionate soul in a family will exert a sweetening and harmonizing influence upon all its members. It is hard to be angry in the presence of imperturbable good-nature. It is well-nigh impossible to be morose in face of a cheerful and generous helpfulness. Beginning with the highest, the ointment drops even upon those who are unconscious or careless of it, and the whole house is presently filled with its fragrance.

Henry Van Dyke

People admire me for my achievements as a business woman.
I know that my greatest achievement was being an
ordinary mom.

Helen Exley

I can't imagine what was so special about being a couple;
being a family is so much nicer.

Alison McWilliams

My dear Mother, the growth of a lifetime is not cut down by absence . . . let me tell you as earnestly and gladly as I can, that I never loved you so devotedly as I do this moment. That every day on which I have delayed to write, you have been before my eyes. . .

That in my happiest hours, my happiness has been incomplete without you.

Edmund Clarence Stedman

Home made jam from mom is really bottled love.

                                        H.M.E.

Mother darling,
It is wonderful to meet and talk over
everything and share and laugh and
understand each other's situations as
no one else can.

Anne Morrow Lindbergh

Mums know whose turn it is to have the skin off the rice pudding, whose turn it is to lick out the cake mix bowl. They know when it's a <u>real</u> stomach ache and when it's physics morning. They know the difference between a bit of fantasizing and a straight lie; between heat rash and measels; between "I Must Have" and "I Want". Solomon was an <u>amateur</u>.

Pam Brown

There is nothing a mother likes better than breakfast in bed — cold toast, burned scrambled egg and a newly-plucked rose dripping dew and greenfly into the cornflakes.

Peter Gray

Mothers know when they are being given a treat – they can hear the fight going on in the kitchen.

Peter Gray

If evolution really works, how come mothers have only two hands?

Ed Dussault

A Chinese proverb tells us that "A hundred men may make an encampment, but it takes a woman to make a home".

A. J. Bucknall

Mothers taken to the theatre when the kids are tiny, 'phone the baby sitter in the interval to see if they are alive and happy. Mothers taken to the theatre when the kids are in their teens 'phone home in the interval to see if it's still standing.

Peter Gray

Nothing looks as lonely as your mom before she sees you coming up the platform.

Pam Brown

Mother love makes a woman more vulnerable than any other creature on earth.

Pam Brown

Mothers need transfusions fairly often – phone calls, letters, bright postcards from the Outer Hebrides.

Heulwen Roberts

*The everlasting sadness of any mother is that there comes a
time when she can no longer bring magic to your life, nor
cure your troubles.*

Diana Briscoe

*It doesn't matter how old I get, whenever I see anything new
or splendid, I want to call "Mum, come and look".*

Helen Thomson

My mom is a lady who has had a lot of problems in her life. Most of them me...
Diana Briscoe

Never tell your kids how well you did at school. Mum still has your reports.

Itoko Fujita

When the son leaves home to start his freshman year at college, his doting mother gives him two cashmere sweaters as going-away presents. Wanting to show his appreciation, the boy comes home for Thanksgiving wearing one of the sweaters. The mother greets him at the door. She takes a long, anxious look and says: "What's the matter. The other sweater you didn't like?".

Liz Smith

No matter how old a mother is, she watches her middle-aged children for signs of improvement.

Florida Scott-Maxwell

The trouble with mothers is that however well groomed and sophisticated you appear to strangers, they know your knickers are probably held up with a safety pin.

Samantha Armstrong

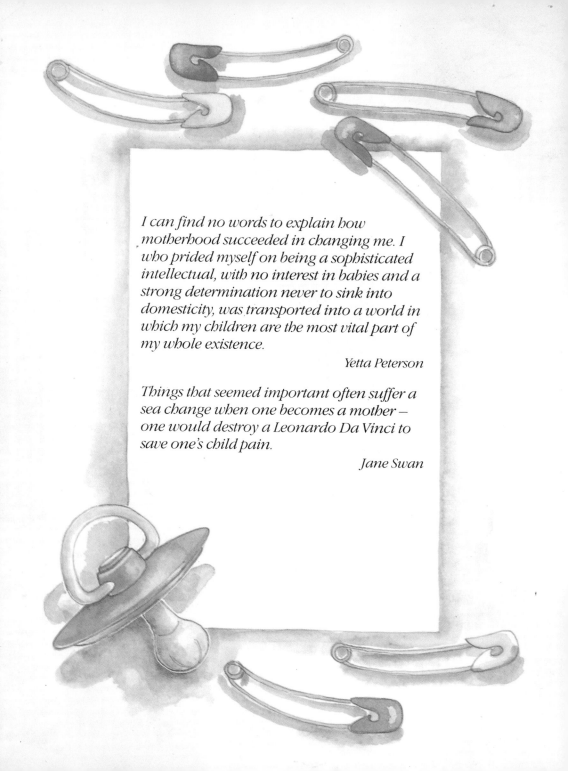

I can find no words to explain how motherhood succeeded in changing me. I who prided myself on being a sophisticated intellectual, with no interest in babies and a strong determination never to sink into domesticity, was transported into a world in which my children are the most vital part of my whole existence.

Yetta Peterson

Things that seemed important often suffer a sea change when one becomes a mother — one would destroy a Leonardo Da Vinci to save one's child pain.

Jane Swan

Fifty-four years of love and tenderness and crossness and devotion and unswerving loyalty. Without her I could only have achieved a quarter of what I have achieved, not only in terms of success and career, but in terms of personal happiness. . . . She has never stood between me and my life, never tried to hold me too tightly, always let me go free. . . .

Noel Coward, about his mother

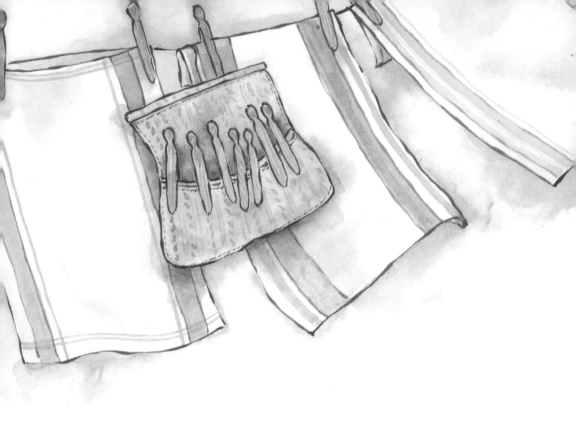

*The more I reflect on the situation of the mother, the more I
am struck with the extent of her powers, and the inestimable
values of her services. In the language of love, women are
called angels; but this is a weak and silly compliment; they
approach nearer to our idea of the Deity: they not only create,
but sustain their creation, and hold its future destiny in their
hands; every man is what his mother made him, and to her he
must be indebted for the greatest blessings in life. . .*
                    William Buchan, from "Advice to Mothers"

Never give your mother a list of presents to choose from. She'll go bankrupt trying to buy them all.

— *Pam Brown*

A mother and her daughter grow closer every time they have a successful shopping spree. Shoes off, kettle on, loot divided. It dates back to the Cave. . .

Samantha Armstrong

One's mom is, to a large extent, a product of one's own imagination – that is why it is so unnerving when they behave like themselves.

Robert E. Judd

BECAUSE SHE IS A MOTHER
She broke the bread into two fragments and gave them to the
children, who ate with avidity.
"She hath kept none for herself," grumbled the Sergeant.
"Because she is not hungry," said a soldier.
"because she is a mother," said the Sergeant.

Victor Hugo

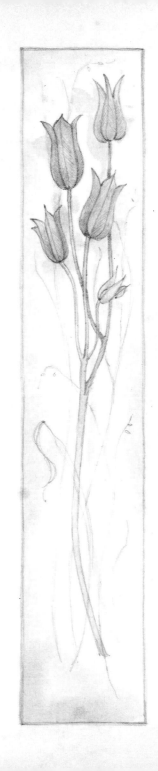

*Whether you like it or not, your mother goes with you.
Forever.*

Helen Exley

All mothers are rich when they love their children.
There are no poor mothers, no ugly ones, no old ones.
Their love is always the most beautiful of the joys.
And when they seem most sad, it needs but a kiss which they
receive or give to turn all their tears into stars. . .

Maurice Maeterlinck

. . . we are still no further away than we ever were and when the pain to see you comes, I don't let it hurt and I don't kill it either for it is the sweetest pain I feel. If sons will go off and marry, or be war correspondents, or managers, it doesn't mean that Home is any less Home. . . . You will never know how much I love you all and you must never give up trying to comprehend it. God bless you and keep you, and my love to you every minute and always.

Richard Harding Davis, from a letter to his mother

Long years you've kept the door ajar
To greet me, coming from afar:
Long years in my accustomed place
I've read my welcome in your face,
And felt the sunlight of your love
Drive back the years and gently move
The telltale shadow 'round to youth,
You've found the very spring, in truth,
That baffles time – the kindly joy
That keeps me in your heart a boy. . .

Robert Bridges

27st marys Gardens
January 23

Darling ma,
Than
your letter, and